Lick

UNTIL THE SUNRISE
#FORCOUPLESONLY

365 NOBLES CONSULTING, LLC

CHERYSE SINGLETON-NOBLES,
CERTIFIED LIFE COACH

LICK UNTIL THE SUNRISE: #FORCOUPLESONLY

AUTHOR: CHERYSE SINGLETON-NOBLES, CERTIFIED LIFE COACH FOR 365 NOBLES CONSULTING, LLC

WWW.365NOBLES.COM
INFO.365NOBLES@GMAIL.COM

ISBN: 978-0-578-72694-6

THIS JOURNAL BELONGS TO MR. & MRS.

ESTABLISHED IN:

COMMITMENT AGREEMENT:

WE PROMISE NOT TO LET OUR DIFFERENCES, TRIALS, TRIBULATIONS, SHORT-COMINGS, MOODS, OR DOWN FALLS STOP US FROM REMEMBERING THE REASON WE GOT MARRIED IN THE FIRST PLACE. INSTEAD, WE PROMISE TO WORK THROUGH IT. WE PROMISE TO REMEMBER TO LAUGH AS WE USE THIS JOURNAL AS A TOOL TO ENJOY OUR MARRIAGE.

(SIGN)

_____

_____

MARRIAGE QUOTES - *page 2*

WRITE YOUR OWN LOVE NOTES - *page 32*

COUPLE ACTIVITIES - *page 44*

Are You Sure You Wanted to Marry Me? I Steal All of the Covers?

Wife: Did you hear what I said?

Husband: Yes.

Wife: What did I say?

Husband: (Silence)

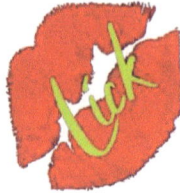

Dear Amazon, Please Deliver My Packages Next Door. My Husband is At Home.

Marriage is like a

workshop where the

husband works and the

wife shops.

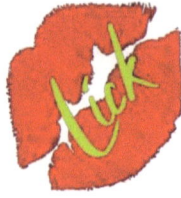

Pause to Reflect on Your

Week Pro's and Con's.

(Hug, Kiss, and Make-up)

Husband: Talk Dirty to me.

Wife: I'm not wearing any

panties because you

didn't do the laundry.

Bride: I do.

Groom: I do what she says.

Marriage is shouting from two different rooms, "Where is the remote?"

Wife: I will never marry you for money. Wait, how much?

Dollar Date Night:

Take this time to be creative and go on a date in a certain part of your house.

Math made simple. Husband if you have $15.00 and your wife has $5.00, she has $20.00.

My wife always has a stash
she thinks I don't know
about.

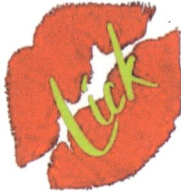

Husband: Okay, Hooters.

Wife: Nope, I don't want that.

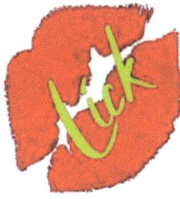

Marriage is falling in love with the same person over and over again. Or is it annoying the same person over and over again?

Marriage allows you to be nasty under the cover...

Oops, did I pass gas?

Don't ever stop flirting with your spouse. Take this time to send a kinky photo, text, or be ready upon arrival.

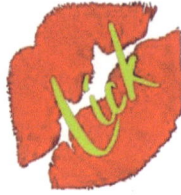

Wife: Downloading now...

Still pending hours later...

Husband: Downloading done.

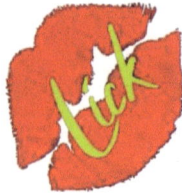

Marriage is 50/50. Where the wife takes the cover 50% of the time.

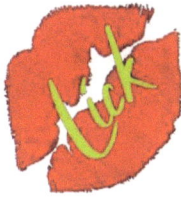

Husband: Whisper sweet nothings.

Wife: Take out the trash.

Love is not having to hold

your farts in anymore.

Married.

What's your superpower?

My husband thinks I'm crazy but I'm not the one who married me.

You call it nagging. I call it,
did you hear me the first
time?

Movie Night:

Take this time to go to the

movies or set the

atmosphere for at home

movie night.

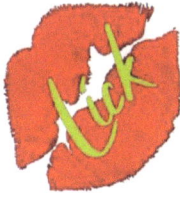

Husbands are the best to share your secrets with. They will never tell anyone because they aren't even listening.

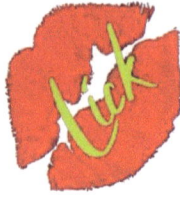

Don't ever laugh at your spouse's choices. You are one of them.

Hot & Spicy:

Take this time to go all the

way out, hot & spicy style.

No need to report my credit
card stolen because my wife
is missing too.

Remember the first rule of marriage. The wife is always right.

Little Love Notes

_____

_____

_____

_____

_____

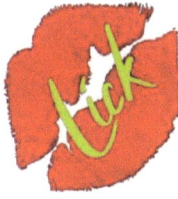

Little Love Notes

_____

_____

_____

_____

_____

Little Love Notes

_____

_____

_____

_____

_____

Little Love Notes

_____

_____

_____

_____

_____

Little Love Notes

_____

_____

_____

_____

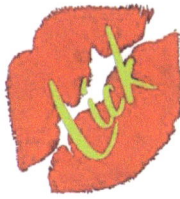

Little Love Notes

_____

_____

_____

_____

_____

Little Love Notes

Little Love Notes

_____

_____

_____

_____

_____

Little Love Notes

_____

_____

_____

_____

_____

Little Love Notes

_____

_____

_____

_____

Little Love Notes

_____

_____

_____

_____

_____

Little Love Notes

COUPLE ACTIVITY:

I Promise to Pull Back the Layers and Love

You Forever.

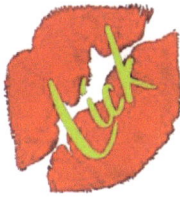

COUPLE ACTIVITY:

Today We Will Lick Until the Sunrise.

COUPLE ACTIVITY:

Today We Will Be In-Between the Sheets.

COUPLE ACTIVITY:

Today We Will Remain Naked All Day.

COUPLE ACTIVITY:

Have It Your Way Today.

COUPLE ACTIVITY:

Today We Will Start Undressing at the Door.

COUPLE ACTIVITY:

Today We Will Lick and Repeat.

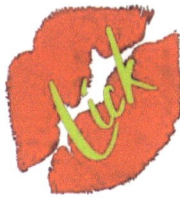

COUPLE ACTIVITY:

Today We Will Remember Why We Fell in

Love in the First Place.

COUPLE ACTIVITY:

Today We Commit to Love.

COUPLE ACTIVITY:

What's Your Position... Start There.

www.ingramcontent.com/pod-product-compliance
Lightning Source LLC
Chambersburg PA
CBHW041218270326
41931CB00001B/26